# Edison

D1510816

## Alexander Kennedy

Amazon.com/author/alexanderkennedy

Copyright 2016 Fritzen Media. All Rights
Reserved.

*No part of this book may be reproduced or
transmitted in any form or by any means, electronic
or mechanical, including photocopying, recording
or by any information storage and retrieval system,
without written permission from the publisher.*

*The information provided within this book is for
general informational purposes only. While we try
to keep the information up-to-date and correct,
there are no representations or warranties, express
or implied, about the completeness, accuracy,
reliability, suitability or availability with respect to
the information, products, services, or related
graphics contained in this book for any purpose.*

# Contents

# Prologue

On January 4, 1903, Coney Island staged one of the most unusual spectacles in its history: the public electrocution of a five-ton, man-killing elephant. A large crowd had assembled to watch the killer meet her fate—newspaper accounts gave its size as anywhere from 1,500 to several thousand people. The execution site, Luna Park, was an amusement park that would open later that year, becoming one of Coney Island's great attractions. That day, however it was still unfinished, a mass of half-constructed "Oriental" buildings that cast long shadows across the fairgrounds. Its mighty cascading fountains had yet to be turned on.

The owners, Frederick Thompson and Elmer Dundy, had originally planned to hang the elephant, known as "Topsy." Shooting an elephant was unreliable and dangerous even with a powerful rifle, and poisonings were easily botched. Most parks that had euthanized elephants in the past had therefore used hanging. Hanging animals for their crimes was in fact a venerable tradition, stretching back to medieval Europe; as late as the American Colonial Era, animals were still being formally tried and hung for killing humans, for participation in bestiality, and for witchcraft.

But Thompson and Dundy were surprised to hear that the American Society for the Prevention of Cruelty to Animals objected to their hanging plan as inhumane. New York State, which had jurisdiction over Coney Island, had recently halted executions of human defendants by hanging in favor of electrocution. Wasn't Topsy entitled to the same consideration, the ASPCA argued?

The ASPCA had been quietly investigating this possibility for years in conjunction with the greatest inventor of his day—and possibly of all time—Thomas Alva Edison. Some years ago, Edison had requested that the ASPCA send him stray dogs that it planned to euthanize by drowning, which was then the society's accepted method. In 1888, he and an assistant, Arthur Kennelly, electrocuted two horses, ten cows, and fifty dogs using alternating current (AC) power. The test subjects (dog lovers might be tempted to say "victims") had a wet bandage wrapped around their foreleg, to which electrified copper wires were applied. Kennelly began with 400 volts and slowly increased the voltage to 1,000 volts, which was generally fatal.

Edison, unsurprisingly, was not conducting these experiments simply out of concern for more painless euthanasia. He had come to them through an odd back channel: a determination to prove that AC power was more dangerous than direct current (DC) power, his preferred method. Edison by this point had mastered the electric light bulb (see Chapter 2), but to build a market, he needed to bring electricity to the cities, the first modern power grid. His great rival in this enterprise was George Westinghouse, and their famous struggle became known as the War of the Currents (see Chapter 3). Westinghouse preferred AC power, and thus Edison set out to discredit it by any means necessary—including demonstrating the dangers of electrocution by AC as publicly and noisily as possible. (DC systems generally used lower voltages, and were therefore safer in this regard.) In one of history's great cases of unintended consequences, the struggle between AC and DC reshaped the face of American capital punishment for a century to come.

By modern standards, Topsy was an unlikely candidate for public execution. She was a minor celebrity, the first elephant ever born in the United States. (Even her name was thoroughly American, taken from the great bestseller of her century, Uncle Tom's Cabin.) Extenuating circumstances abounded in the "murder" she had committed. Topsy had been with the Forepaugh & Sells Brothers Circus when a drunk named James Fielding Blount had pushed into the tent where the elephants were chained up. After taunting them and attempting to make them drink whiskey, he had deliberately burnt the tip of Topsy's trunk—one of the most sensitive parts of an elephant's body—with a lit cigar. Topsy knocked Blount to the ground, stomped on him with one foot, and crushed him into the sawdust, killing him instantly.

For a year or so, the circus continued to tour with Topsy, using the killing for publicity. Topsy had killed four men, the advertisements claimed, or twelve—the number didn't really matter, as long as people kept buying tickets. But when another man jabbed Topsy with a stick and she attempted to kill him as well, the circus had second thoughts about its approach. It sold Topsy at a discount to the owners of the new Luna Park. These new owners couldn't control her, either, and after a remarkable incident in which Topsy attempted to batter down the doors of a police station—her handler had been arrested for drunkenness—they resolved to kill her.

So that cold January day, at least 1,500 spectators filed into the fairgrounds, paying twenty-five cents a head to see Topsy die. Thompson and Dundy had flooded the newspapers with planted reports and advertisements for days, seeing the publicity value for Luna Park. They chose the area beside their new "Electric Tower"—two hundred feet tall and covered in electric lights—for their spectacle. Now the tower was fitted out with large ropes that would be used to restrain and strangle Topsy during her electrocution. Signs at its base read "OPENING MAY 2ND 1903 LUNA PARK $1,000,000 EXPOSITION, THE HEART OF CONEY ISLAND."

Contrary to later legend, Thomas Edison himself was not present to supervise the execution. There is no definitive proof of his whereabouts, but it would have been strange if every newspaperman covering the event—which had become a national story—had failed to note the presence of one of America's most famous men. Still, Edison's fingerprints were everywhere, as they were in every American city of his day. The Electric Tower was covered in light bulbs of his design; the Edison Electric Illuminating Company had spent the whole night rerouting power lines from a substation nine blocks away; and a film crew from the Edison Film Company was on hand to record the proceedings.

The copyright on this one-minute, seventeen-second movie has long since expired, and it can be watched in its entirety on YouTube. It begins with Topsy being led from her pen toward the "gallows," wearing a martingale harness to partially restrain her. The film cuts ahead at the twenty-second mark; Topsy had balked at a bridge across a small moat and refuse to advance farther. Her former handler was in the audience, the one whom Topsy had tried to rescue from the police station, but he refused an offer of $25 to coax her to her death, saying he would not do it even for a thousand. Instead, the executioners had to move their whole apparatus to the elephant. She was harnessed in and then fed a bushel of poisoned carrots—her owners were taking no chances in front of this large a crowd.

The film resumes. Topsy stamps one foot, confused and alarmed by these events, odd even by circus and amusement park standards. At exactly 2:45, chief electrician P.D. Sharkey gave a command into the telephone for a man at the substation to throw the switch. At the 39-second mark of the film, Topsy gives a sudden start. Smoke begins to rise from beneath her, and she topples two seconds later, her legs stiff as 6,600 volts course through her enormous body. The smoke engulfs her, and for a moment, she is hidden from view. A man passes cheerfully before the camera. After ten seconds, the voltage shuts off, and the smoke begins to clear. Topsy is not moving. A man steps forward to supervise as the nooses around her neck are tightened by steam winches. Though she appears quite dead already, these nooses will strangle her for the next ten minutes—again, the owners were taking no chances. The film mercifully cuts out after only a few seconds of this, the nooses still taut around her neck.

This episode, so inglorious to modern eyes, nonetheless encapsulates many elements of Edison's protean career. It demonstrates how rapidly his inventions were changing the face of American society, for one. Luna Park had his light bulbs on all its buildings, and the tallest structure, Electric Tower, implicitly celebrated his achievements; already electric light was considered an indispensable accompaniment to the gaiety of an amusement park. When Thompson and Dundy needed electricity for the electrocution, it was to Edison's power company they turned, and the very concept of electrocution had come from Edison's research. (Edison just missed his chance to name it as well. He had proposed "electromort," "dynamort," or "ampermort"; one of his lawyers, pressing the Westinghouse connection to the extreme, suggested referring to electrocuting someone as "westinghousing" him.) And one of Edison's pioneering cameras was there to record the event, and the resulting film was soon added to the rotation in his "Kinetoscope" exhibition devices.

But this film also provided Edison with bad publicity in the long run. The title, "Electrocuting an Elephant—Thomas A.

Edison," gave the false impression that Edison was far more involved in Topsy's death than he was. Even today, respected magazines such as Wired and Business Insider print inaccurate stories suggesting Edison arranged the elephant's death as part of "The War of the Currents," which Edison had already lost quite definitively a decade before—AC power was already the standard and remains so to this day. This, too, is typical of Edison's public image; once considered one of the great American heroes, he is now commonly portrayed as the villain in his rivalries with competitors, most notably the eccentric Serbian-American scientist Nikola Tesla. The urban legends around Edison, as in the case of poor Topsy, therefore tend to be negative and even malicious.

The following book attempts to sort out fact from fiction in the life of this iconic American, scraping away a century of legends to get at the real Edison: neither hero nor villain, sometimes a saint and sometimes a sinner, but always a genius, and one whose inventions continue to shape every day of our lives.

# Introduction

Thomas Edison's greatest contribution to society was not his inventions, but his unique process of taking existing ideas and improving upon them until they reached their most practical state. For example, despite what many think, Thomas Edison did not invent the electric light bulb. Many earlier inventors had produced incandescent bulbs, but they were useful only as demonstrations of the practicality of producing light via electricity. Edison's patent for the electric light bulb was for an improved incandescent bulb, which made it a commercially marketable product.

Edison reinvented the process of invention itself. He developed the world's first research and development laboratory, in which the work of others was combined, studied, and advanced. He used telegraphy to develop what became the phonograph. He studied the art and science of photography to develop motion picture photography, creating a new science, art, and industry. His team of employees and assistants were issued over 1,000 patents in his name during his lifetime. He became world famous for his achievements before he was forty years old.

Due to his fame, he was highly sought for interview. He made many errors of judgment throughout his career, and did not discuss them comfortably, preferring to focus on his many successes. He developed rivalries, most notably with Nikola Tesla, which are still studied today. Many of these studies depict Edison as an almost evil figure and Tesla as a noble saint. This was not the case.

Edison invented industries and products and new ways to spend leisure time. Many of these will remain in demand long after the incandescent bulb falls into total disuse. The music player industry began with his phonograph, the motion picture industry with his kinetescope, and the telephone was made practical through his improvements to its receiver. His life's work has made life in the 21st century significantly better.

# Chapter 1:
# The Young
# Entrepreneur

Thomas Alva Edison was born in the village of Milan, Ohio on February 11, 1847. The United States had recently acquired vast new western lands through the Treaty of Guadalupe Hidalgo, which ended the Mexican-American War and stretched American territory to the shores of the Pacific Ocean. The nation had entered a period of prosperity and rapid industrial growth. Milan prospered as a shipping center. Grain from the fertile fields of northern Ohio arrived at the town via wagon, and was transferred to canal boats that carried it up the Milan and Erie Canal to the Huron river, and finally to eastern ports. The village bustled with boatyards and visiting boatmen, waggoneers, and sailors.

The young Edison — called Al by family and friends — was the seventh child born to his parents, Samuel and Nancy Edison. Three of his siblings died in childhood. Edison's surviving siblings were much older than he, and he was raised largely as an only child. His father was a political exile from Canada who worked in Milan as a shingler, cutting wood shingles for houses and other buildings. His mother was a former schoolteacher. In his early years, Edison was exposed to books from his father's extensive library, which offered the firebrand political philosophy his father had practiced in Canada, along with books on mechanics, chemistry, and Newtonian Principles.

# Edison's Early Childhood

Edison developed hearing problems at an early age, which likely contributed to him being regarded as a slow child. Edison later told conflicting tales of how these difficulties developed. In one, he attributed it to an injury as a result of one of his experiments gone awry, and in another he blamed them on an incident in which he was lifted by his ears. More likely, his hearing problems developed as a result of ear infections from swimming in the dirty waters of the canal, a pastime enjoyed by the boys of Milan.

Edison displayed an insatiable curiosity about how things worked and a desire to build things from whatever materials came to hand. The boatyards and grain warehouses provided plenty of resources for him, and were his source of scrap wood. Edison used this scrap to construct miniature plank roads and other projects.

His curiosity and industry got him into trouble from time to time. Once he started a fire in a barn because he wanted to know which woods would burn the longest. The fire rapidly grew out of control, burned down the barn, and earned him a public spanking in the village square as a deterrence to others. In another incident he later recalled, he was attacked by a ram while preoccupied by trying to dig into a beehive, evidently in a quest for honey. The ram butted him into the fence post that housed the beehive.

# Moving to Port Huron and Edison's Education

The year of Edison's birth proved to be the height of Milan's prosperity. By the early 1850's, the canal era was ending in the United States. The bulk of shipping from the interior was shifting to the railroads, which had bypassed the village. When Edison was seven years old, the family relocated to Port Huron, Michigan.

Edison's formal education in Port Huron began and ended in just three months. His mother withdrew him from school after learning that his teacher there had referred to him as "addled." From then on, his mother assumed responsibility for Edison's schooling, and the books in his father's library helped him learn. Edison never mastered mathematics and thought little of it, and later said "I can always hire some mathematicians, but they can't hire me." Edison's reading was encouraged by his father, who paid the boy for each book he completed.

The Edison home was situated on ten acres of land, and supported a large garden, which the youngster began working at the age of eleven, raising and selling vegetables to help with the family's finances. Although Edison enjoyed the commercial aspects of this enterprise, he was not fond of the agricultural work.

Although Edison achieved fame primarily through the application of electricity, in his youth he showed little interest in the subject, and preferred to study and experiment with chemistry. He acquired, over the next few years, a large and complex collection of chemicals and equipment with which he experimented in the basement of the family home, to the frequent dismay of his mother, who objected to the often noxious smells permeating through the house. His limited allowance eventually grew insufficient to support his desire for more chemicals and equipment, and he had by then read through his father's library. He decided to apply for a position as a newsboy, selling newspapers on the trains which ran between Port Huron and Detroit.

## Early Business Ventures

It didn't take long for Edison to recognize and exploit the marketing opportunities presented by the expanding rail service between Detroit and Port Huron. Vegetables from the area around Port Huron were of higher quality than those available in Detroit, and were cheaper. Edison bought produce in Port Huron, sold them in Detroit, and made a tidy profit. He transported them in a baggage car, half of which was supposed to be dedicated to the US Mail. When the propriety of using a mail car for commerce was questioned, he offered vegetables to railroad officials' wives at cost — essentially bribing them— demonstrating an astute grasp of human nature.

By fifteen, Edison was writing, publishing, and distributing his own newspaper, which he named the Weekly Herald, and he employed other boys to continue his vegetable enterprise. He set up his chemical apparatus in the baggage car, but was soon evicted from it after a chemical spill set the car on fire. He also became fascinated by telegraphy, and often watched the electromechanical machines in railway telegraph offices with rapt attention.

# Edison Learns of the Power of the Telegraph

In April of 1862, the news of the Battle of Shiloh and its appalling casualties appeared in Detroit newspapers. Edison had the headlines announcing the casualties and the uncertain nature of the battle's outcome telegraphed to the stations along the line to Port Huron. He then negotiated with the editors of the Detroit Free Press to obtain one thousand copies of the edition with the latest news of the battle. With hundreds of Michigan volunteers serving in the Union Army, Edison knew that the demand for information would be great. At each station on the line, he found crowds clamoring for the latest news, and sold the newspapers at a large profit before reaching Port Huron. He was just fifteen years old.

When Edison prevented the son of one of the railway's telegraphers from being seriously injured in an accident, the grateful father took it upon himself to teach Edison the basics of the telegraph key. Within weeks, Edison had his first position as a professional telegraph operator, and worked the night shift in Stratford Junction, Ontario.

# The Professional Telegrapher

Over the next five years, he hopped from position to position, in Michigan, Kentucky, Ohio, Tennessee, and Indiana. He developed a great ability as a receiver, but was not as talented a sender. He was well regarded by his peers, fellow operators mostly of similar age, and demonstrated a taste for practical jokes. While working in Cincinnati, he and an associate wired a sink in the men's washroom to a powerful induction coil he had purchased, and they watched through a hole drilled in the roof as victim after victim received shocks when they attempted to wash their hands. "We enjoyed the sport immensely," Edison commented later.

By 1868, Edison was in Boston, working as an accomplished telegrapher who tinkered endlessly with the apparatus of his trade. His experience had taught him that there was a need for several improvements in telegraphy, such as improved transmitters, and that the technology could be applied to other uses, including an electric vote recorder which could be marketed to government for legislatures, a stock price recorder, and fire alarms.

## Early Inventions

Edison soon found that the government did not favor recorders that could speed up the voting process, and although Edison had obtained a patent for the device — his first — it had no market. From this experience, Edison determined that commercial viability, not technical advancement, should be the motivation behind invention. The stock ticker seemed to meet this requirement. He took his invention, and began offering a service. Soon he had nearly forty subscribers. The success of this device soon drew Edison's attention to the larger markets in New York. A trip there in 1868 failed to generate much interest in his stock ticker, and Edison returned to Boston, where he began to develop a duplex telegraph — a device which would allow two messages to be sent simultaneously over a single line. To market this device, he left his employment with Western Union and journeyed to New York City, the hub of the world of telegraphy.

## The Professional Inventor

By then, Edison had decided what the course of his life and career would be, and that his days as a sender and receiver of telegraph messages while in the employ of another were over. His goal was to own a shop in which he could develop and manufacture improved telegraph equipment to paying customers. To achieve this, he sought financial backing. New York contained the headquarters of Western Union and the Gold and Stock Telegraph Company, both potentially lucrative customers for the devices he wished to produce.

Edison partnered with Franklin Leonard Pope, a leading telegraph engineer. Together they developed a series of printing telegraphs and formed three separate businesses to market them. Over the course of the next several months, Edison's reputation amongst major players in the telegraph industry became such that the Gold and Stock Telegraph Company contracted him to produce a facsimile system.

The money from the facsimile contract enabled Edison and his new partner— a mechanic named William Unger— to open a manufacturing shop across the river in Newark New Jersey. It also enabled Edison to devote some of his time to other projects, including an idea for a high-speed telegraph which used punched paper tape to transmit rather than Morse code keyed manually. Over the course of the next five years, Edison established his reputation as a telegraph inventor, and numerous companies bid for control of his work. By October of 1870, Edison had formed the American Telegraph Works. The following May, he contracted as a consulting electrician and mechanic for the Gold and Stock Telegraph Company.

The automatic system led Edison to develop multiple telegraph systems, and by 1874 he successfully demonstrated a quadruplex system capable of transmitting four messages at a time, two in each direction. Later that year, he signed a contract with Western Union that granted his work in multiple telegraphy to the company.

By 1875, Edison was widely esteemed within the telegraph industry in the United States and Great Britain. The number of his patented inventions continued to grow. Without any formal education in engineering, electricity, mechanics, or business he had established a successful career as a consultant and inventor. When he needed expertise outside of his own, he had the wherewithal to hire it, and his shops were staffed with highly skilled artisans and mechanics.

# Marriage and the Decision to Cease Manufacturing

One of Edison's companies had a particularly lasting impact on Edison's life. In 1871, Edison and Unger formed the News Reporting Telegraph Company with the idea to transmit business news directly to businessmen. They transmitted the news to business people prior to it appearing in the newspapers, giving their customers access to news as it broke.

Among the employees Edison and Unger hired for this venture was a 16-year-old girl named Mary Stillwell. In December 1871, Mary and Edison were married, and shortly thereafter they moved into a new home in Newark.

Edison also began searching for a product that he could mass-market to consumers outside the limited telegraph industry. In 1874, he produced the Inductorium, a battery-powered device that produced electric shocks, which was marketed as a cure for rheumatism. It sold well enough that Edison's name began to become known outside of the world of telegraphy, although its ability to cure rheumatism is doubtful.

By 1875, Edison had had his fill of manufacturing. His goal was to pursue invention and research on a full-time basis. He preferred to license other manufacturers to produce the products and live off the royalties. Edison began scouting locations for a research and development facility, and found a suitable place in New Jersey, about 30 miles from New York. The site consisted of about thirty homes situated on large lots, with unpaved streets except for a central wooden boardwalk. The site had neither a school nor a church, but it did have a train station and a saloon. It was known as Menlo Park, and it later launched his rise to fame.

# Chapter 2:

# Menlo Park

Just prior to moving his workshop to Menlo Park, Edison invented a device he called the electric pen. It mechanically perforated tape. The device was intended to be marketed to the public and generate lucrative profits. The pen, connected to a battery, featured a rapidly moving needle which was used to create a master stencil, from which copies could be reproduced — a forerunner of the mimeograph.

It was not a success. Customers complained that trying to hold the needle down on paper was difficult, and that the pen generated excessive vibration. It found modest success when it was reinvented more than a decade later as the first electric tattoo needle.

Edison licensed the duplicating technology to Albert Blake Dick, a lumber merchant. Through his company, The AB Dick Company, the pen was marketed as the Edison

Mimeograph. AB Dick became the world's largest manufacturer of mimeograph equipment, though not from sales of the electric pen. Dick was the founder of the quick printing industry, operating storefronts to produce multiple copies of documents on demand. Although the electric pen was a commercial disappointment for Edison, it was the gateway to a whole new means of doing business.

Edison was unconcerned with the manufacturing and distribution problems of the electric pen, other than to note its disappointing sales performance. Menlo Park was by then the full focus of his attention. The little hamlet was a failed real estate development so small that its train station lacked a sign designating the place. The three story house closest to the station had been the real estate sales office, and became the Edison residence. By then, the Edisons had two children, a daughter named Marion, born in 1873, and a son, Thomas Alva Edison Jr., who arrived in 1876. Edison called Marion "Dot" and Thomas Jr. "Dash," references to the Morse code that had been so influential to him.

Edison spent nearly $3,000 to build his laboratory, which was situated on a rise above the residence. Edison hired his father to do the construction, and paid him with money from Jay Gould and Western Union. The laboratory was an elongated two story building, with telegraph wires from the train station entering it on the second floor. Although Edison had been searching for products that held mass appeal, telegraphy remained his bread and butter.

Edison established yet another company, the American Novelty Company, for the purpose of marketing the non-telegraphic ideas that grew out of the laboratory, including the electric pen. Some of these products were an electric drill, a jewelry engraving machine, an electric shearer to harvest wool from sheep, and others. The American Novelty Company closed in less than a year, having failed to generate much in the way of marketable products.

# Working at Menlo Park

Many of the ideas which arose within the laboratory came from intense discussion sessions of a nature that is now referred to as brainstorming. Edison himself participated in some of the sessions, but many were conducted by his assistants in his absence, such as when his attention was drawn to a different project. Edison had long before decided that he would work on what he wanted, when he wanted, and he conducted himself accordingly.

The assistants that he hired soon learned that the working hours at Menlo Park varied according to the whims of the boss. Normal working hours were eight hours a day, Monday through Saturday. However, whenever Edison worked late, his assistants were expected to work as well. Edison was capable of multiple-day spurts, during which he would not leave the laboratory, refreshing himself with catnaps at his desk or sprawled across a workbench. The frequency of these all-night sessions increased whenever it became evident that they were closing in on success for a given project.

To fuel these all-night sessions, Edison served dinner in the laboratory at midnight. No midnight snack, these dinners were large, heavy meals, and were served to the men as they sat together around a dining table in a convivial atmosphere. Rather than working dinners with discussion centered on the problems that kept them working late, conversation was of a fraternal, club-like nature. These dinners would frequently run on for some time until, in the words of one employee, "Edison arose, stretched, took a hitch at his waist band in sailor fashion and began to saunter away – the signal that dinner was over, and it was time to begin work again."

# Staffing and Stocking the Laboratory

Edison's management style allowed work to go forward on multiple projects simultaneously, with his involvement in each varying in accordance with his interest. Many of the patents which bear Edison's name were the result of combined efforts between Edison and his assistants, though they all bore his name.

Edison staffed Menlo Park with highly skilled experts in their fields. He demonstrated a knack for identifying talent. One such expert was William Joseph Hammer, who Edison hired as a laboratory assistant in December 1879. Hammer later became indispensable in the development of the improved incandescent light bulb. Another significant hire was Edison's Chief Assistant, Charles W. Batchelor, a draftsman and mechanic who would become Edison's closest associate and good friend. It was Batchelor who introduced a young Nikola Tesla to Edison via a letter of introduction.

Edison gave his key assistants shares in the various companies created by his products, and encouraged them to invest further with their own capital. Many of the companies he created, including the Edison Electric Light Company, the Edison Lamp Company, and the Edison Machine Works proved highly profitable, increasing the income of his assistants far beyond the salaries they earned for their work at Menlo Park.

This generosity with stock options was a way to offset the reputation Edison had for paying relatively low salaries, given the demands of the work schedule. Edison was forced to keep salaries low due to the lack of income from his many inventions.

# Multitasking and the Phonograph

Edison's involvement with multiple projects allowed him to extract ideas from one project and insert them into another, which helped some projects move forward. His employees were also moved around frequently. Often, as one project moved closer to fruition, talent was transferred from one group to another to focus on the solution. It was this method of sharing talent between groups that helped devise the invention that first rocketed Edison to fame — the phonograph.

Edison had been working on two seemingly unrelated projects. "I was experimenting on an automatic method of recording telegraph messages on a disk of paper laid on a revolving platen..." while at the same time in another area of the lab, work progressed on improvements to Alexander Graham Bell's new telephone. Bell's telephone lacked a microphone sufficient to transmit the human voice clearly and accurately reproduce its sound over distances. Edison, who had been working on a telephone of his own and had been closer to success than he realized, began looking at ways to improve the microphone. His solution was the carbon transmitter, which was so successful it was used in telephones as recently as the 1980s.

Combining information extracted from the two separate projects, Edison realized that the vibrations detected by the carbon transmitter could be transferred to a needle, which could then etch them onto a physical medium, such as paper or tinfoil. When reversed, the etchings would vibrate the needle, and eventually the carbon transmitter. After some brainstorming, Edison and his assistants produced what he referred to as a "talking-machine."

A functioning phonograph was completed by July 1877, during an overnight session at Menlo Park. A cylinder rotated with a hand crank, and the electricity required for its operation came from electromagnets. Edison did not at first recognize the potential commercial applications for the device. To Edison, the talking machine was still tied to the limited market of telegraphy rather than mass consumption.

On December 7, 1877, Edison showed up at the New York offices of Scientific American, set up a small phonograph on an editor's desk, and started cranking. The machine announced itself by saying "How do you do?" Scientific

American delayed publication of its next issue to include the announcement of the phonograph.

Edison's days of working in obscurity were over from that moment. He was soon barraged with requests for interviews from the press in nearby New York and Philadelphia, who visited Menlo Park. The reporters did not limit their pieces to their impressions of the phonograph, but also described the activities there, estimating the number of inventions in progress at somewhere in the hundreds. Edison quickly became known to the public as the Wizard of Menlo Park.

Edison pushed the phonograph's development as a business tool for both telegraphy and office dictation rather than for entertainment purposes. By the time he was persuaded to market it for mass appeal, its technology had been surpassed by others who used more convenient and longer playing discs as the recording medium instead of cylinders. Despite its impact on the press and the public, who regarded the phonograph and its inventor with awe, it did not bring Edison financial rewards for some time.

# The Incandescent Light Bulb

In the spring of 1878, after he personally demonstrated the phonograph to President Benjamin Hayes in Washington DC, Edison returned to Menlo Park and began development of a practical incandescent lamp. Edison formed the Edison Electric Light Company in New York City with the financial backing of J.P. Morgan and others. His research continued, with experimentation focusing on the materials to use as the filament. A wide range was tested, including carbon, platinum, carbonized cotton, bamboo and others. Eventually, they returned to carbon, and by

November of 1879 they had produced a bulb which burned continuously for 13 ½ hours. This design was patented as "a carbon filament or strip coiled and connected to platina contact wires." On New Year's Eve in 1879, Edison demonstrated what he described as the first practical incandescent bulb at Menlo Park, announcing, "We will make electricity so cheap that only the rich will burn candles." Development of new filaments did not stop, however, and within a few months of that announcement they created a carbonized bamboo filament that burned for nearly 1200 hours.

One of the attendees at the demonstration was Henry Villard, president of the Oregon Railroad and Navigation Company. Edison had long pursued Villard as a potential investor in his inventions. Villard's company was building a new steamship, the Columbia, which was nearing completion. Villard, recognizing a marketing opportunity, asked Edison to install electric lighting on his new ship. In May of 1880, Edison personally supervised the installation of Columbia's lighting system — the first commercial application of the incandescent light bulb.

The phonograph and the incandescent light bulb made him and his laboratory at Menlo Park world famous. The little hamlet was quickly besieged with visitors seeking demonstrations of both. Edison began to expand the facility, hiring the New York City engineering firm Babcock and Wilcox to build a machine shop behind the existing laboratory building. He also built a separate office and library for his own use. He remodeled an existing wooden building opposite the railroad tracks to serve as his lamp factory. One of his assistants, a mathematician named Francis Upton, had the distinction of owning the first home to be entirely lit with incandescent bulbs, and others soon followed.

Edison developed the dynamo, which provided a continuous and stable DC current that could be distributed to multiple buildings, as a preliminary to providing incandescent light to urban areas. The dynamo, like nearly all of Edison's inventions, was an improvement on existing technology. In this case, it expanded upon the work of Michael Faraday half a century before.

Other work at Menlo Park included the development of an electrical railway which ran from the machine shop to a site about three blocks north, and which proved that electricity was a suitable means of locomotion. By September 1882, at the age of 35, Edison's incandescent light had been fitted into all the homes and office buildings on Pearl Street in downtown New York.

# Conflicts Threaten Growth

With his growing fame and success, Edison found that he had less time to be actively involved in the research conducted in his laboratory, as he was pressed by businessmen and investors. He also began battling litigation. In 1883, Edison's patent on the incandescent bulb was ruled invalid by the US patent office, which said it had been based on the previous work of William Sawyer. This litigation stretched on for six years before a judge overturned the patent office's decision. During this period, Edison entered into a business arrangement with British inventor Joseph Swan, who had been awarded a patent in England for an incandescent bulb a year before Edison received his. Rather than go into litigation, the two inventors formed a company, which they called Ediswan, to manufacture and market the light bulb in Great Britain.

Joseph Swan had demonstrated a practical incandescent prior to Edison in 1878, but did not patent it until 1880. Swan was also the first to light a public building with electric light. He had developed a filament made of cellulose, which became the industry standard for all but the Edison Company, which continued to use the bamboo derivative filament until 1892.

During his time in Menlo Park, Edison, true to his nature, developed marketable products based on the improvement of existing technology. Both his phonograph and his electric light borrowed from the knowledge he had acquired in his work to improve telegraphy. The phonograph was invented because of Edison's desire to record the sounds of telegraphy in order to increase the speed at which messages could be translated. His use and experience with telegraphy, which relied on low voltage DC power largely from batteries, is undoubtedly why he used low voltage DC power in developing the incandescent lamp.

Edison's shifted his focus to increase the marketability of the electric lamp by creating an electric utility to distribute electrical power and compete directly with gas lighting utilities. The creation of electrical power and its safe distribution was necessary in order to maintain sales of his light bulb.

As he met with politicians and investors in pursuit of this utility, Edison spent less time at Menlo Park, and by 1881 he no longer resided there, although he and his family returned in the summers. During Edison's tenure at Menlo Park, which he dubbed "the Invention Factory," more than 400 patents were issued in his name.

# Chapter 3:
# The War of the Currents

In 1882, Thomas Edison established the Edison Illuminating Company in New York City with the intent to compete with established gas utilities, who were then the leading supplier of illumination to businesses and residences. He also competed with arc lamp utilities. Arc lamp systems were mostly powered by alternating current, and so the majority of existing electrical distribution systems were based on AC. Arc lamps emitted garish and uneven light, and were deemed unsuitable for use in residences. The high-voltage AC systems which powered the arc lights were also considered dangerous to work on.

The sheer number of dynamos required to generate the direct current for the Edison Illuminating Company was beyond the capacity of the workshops at Menlo Park. Edison established the Edison Machine Works on Manhattan's lower east side to address this issue.

In June of 1884, Edison was approached by an urbane Croatian electrical engineer who carried a letter of introduction from Charles Batchelor. The young man had worked for Continental Edison in France, and was seeking employment in the United States. His name was Nikola Tesla. Edison hired Tesla to work at the Edison Machine Works, and was tasked with redesigning the Edison Company's direct current generators. According to Tesla, he was offered a $50,000 bonus if he could improve the inefficient generators. When Tesla completed the work in a few months, he asked about the payment, and was told by Edison, "Tesla, you don't understand our American humor." Offered a $10 per week raise by Edison, Tesla refused and resigned. There were more conflicts to come.

# DC vs. AC

The DC system favored by Edison had a major drawback: it was suitable only for densely populated areas. It had the advantage of being safer, as AC power had to be transmitted at very high voltages. By the mid-1880s, however, an AC system owned by Westinghouse Electric was developed that could transmit AC current over long distances, on relatively thin wires. The current was then stepped down to lower voltages for distribution through transformers. By contrast, the DC system required much heavier copper wires for transmission, which were both more expensive and difficult to work with. The ability to step down the AC transmission made it suitable not only for street and outdoor lighting but also for use indoors. Westinghouse had also developed a slightly altered incandescent light bulb which used AC but did not infringe upon Edison's patents.

Despite the drawbacks, Edison continued to move forward with DC systems, despite noted progress in the ability of AC systems to deliver power safely and more cheaply. The AC system also allowed power stations to be well removed from residential areas, while DC required that dynamos be within the area in which the power was distributed. The DC powerhouses were often a public nuisance, as they were noisy and emitted noxious fumes in the neighborhood.

By late 1887, Edison had 121 DC power generation stations, Westinghouse had 68 AC stations, and the Thomson-Houston Electric Company (which offered both AC and DC) had 22 stations. Several other smaller companies existed around the country, all with their own power systems, arc lighting, incandescent bulb designs, and support equipment, which led to continuous legal wrangling and patent battles between each other and with Edison. Edison also began to encounter resistance to the DC system, and members of his companies urged him to convert to an AC system. He remained staunchly opposed to AC, however, and continued to champion the DC system.

In the mid-1880s, Edison established a pattern of attacking the proponents of AC on a personal level, including George Westinghouse, when he stated, "Just as certain as death, Westinghouse will kill a customer within six months after he puts in a system of any size."

Edison possessed an in-depth knowledge of how AC systems worked, and remained of the opinion that DC was a more cost-efficient system. When he could not find a reason for other companies to use DC because of his perceptions, he concluded that Westinghouse and Thomson-Houston were using AC systems only as a means to avoid violating Edison's patents. He decided that an educated public would come to the realization that he was correct. He thus began a campaign to both tout the Edison DC system and to point out the inadequacies and dangers of the competing AC system. He relied on the esteem in which he was held by the general public as the miracle inventor the Wizard of Menlo Park.

# Attacks on Alternating Current

In the summer of 1888, Harold Brown, an electrical engineer, published a letter to the editor in the New York Post in which he stated clearly that the more dangerous AC system was being used because it provided utilities with a less expensive system, increasing their profit margins. These attacks were again directed against George Westinghouse, and they helped create a public image of a profiteer indifferent to the dangers to which the public was exposed. George Westinghouse responded to these personal attacks by inviting Edison to visit him, and in a letter to Edison he stated, "I believe there has been a systemic attempt on the part of some people to do a great deal of mischief and create as great a difference as possible between the Edison Company and The Westinghouse Electric Company..." Edison declined the invitation.

Instead Edison offered his assistance to Brown and the use of space and equipment in Edison's laboratory, then located in West Orange New Jersey. He also assigned laboratory assistant Arthur Kennelly to assist Brown in his experiments.

## The Brown Experiments

Using stray dogs which Brown paid children to collect, Brown conducted a series of experiments during which he jolted the dogs with both AC and DC current. Brown held a public demonstration on July 30th at Columbia, during which he applied a series of shocks to a dog at increasing voltages using DC current. The dog survived shocks of up to 1000 volts. A single shock using AC current at 330 volts killed the dog. Using the data he obtained from this and subsequent experiments, Brown began to lobby state legislatures to limit AC current to 300 volts, a level which would render it unable to compete with Edison's DC system.

George Westinghouse meanwhile pursued the goal of a completely integrated AC system by purchasing several competitors outright. He also obtained the rights for an AC induction motor — patented by Nikola Tesla — an important step toward an integrated system. Edison responded by consolidating on his own; the Edison Lamp Company, Edison Machine Works, and the Edison Electric Light Company merged under the new name of The Edison General Electric Company. This merger was backed financially with the help of Drexel and J. P. Morgan and Co., and Henry Villard was installed as president.

Brown's public experiments convinced the State of New York to hire him as a consultant, and he was tasked with recommending the current that would be best applied in the development of an electric chair for the execution of criminals. Brown again contacted Edison to request the use of the West Orange laboratory to conduct tests on animals that were larger than a human. Thomas Edison was a witness to Brown's experiments, which all used alternating current, and included the execution of four calves and a horse at 750 volts.

Brown published an article detailing the experiment entitled "The Comparative Danger to Life of the Alternating and Continuous Electrical Current" in the form of a 61 page booklet which was paid for by Edison General Electric. Later that spring, New York executed its first criminal in the electric chair, which generated extended newspaper discussion over what the new form of execution should be called. A lawyer working for Edison wrote that Edison believed Westinghouse was the best choice.

# Westinghouse and Tesla Respond

In 1889, four linemen in New York City and one in Buffalo were killed in accidents involving high-voltage AC lines. The deaths induced panic over the idea of high-voltage lines ranging overhead in crowded cities, and the recent acquisition of multiple power distribution companies by Westinghouse caused the focus of the public blame to shift to him. A proposal was put forth to bury all electrical power lines underground.

In a November of that year, in an article he published in the North American Review titled "The Dangers of Electric Lighting," Edison denounced AC current as deadly. In response to the suggestion that public safety would be enhanced by burying AC transmission lines underground, eliminating the danger from overhead wires, Edison stated that such a move would be a constant menace. Edison insisted that AC could never be made safe unless its voltage was limited, and stated bluntly that Edison General Electric would never adopt AC power while he was in charge of the company. He implied that Westinghouse was aware of the danger, which placed Westinghouse in a position in which he appeared to be prioritizing profits over public safety.

Westinghouse responded a month later in a letter published in the North American Review. He simply pointed out that his AC step down transformer system delivered lower voltages than Edison's DC system.

Regardless of the propaganda attacks on Westinghouse and the AC system, AC began to dominate DC as the preferred choice for electrical utilities. When it became clear that a system using Tesla's induction motor in a fully integrated AC system could generate enough power at Niagara Falls to ensure electrical distribution throughout the Northeast United States — a range a DC station could not possibly cover — DC's market share plummeted. Westinghouse and Tesla's AC system was selected to light the Columbian Exhibition in Chicago, an event which represented more than 40 countries and which clearly demonstrated AC's superiority and safety.

The Edison Company's loss of market share and smaller profits than either Westinghouse or Thomson-Houston began to generate discomfort amongst shareholders over Edison's leadership. Edison General Electric engineers and scientists began to clamor more loudly for conversion to AC. Edison's efforts to educate the public on the dangers of AC and the superiority of his DC system had not worked.

# The Creation of General Electric

Edison no longer had majority control after the 1889 merger formed Edison General Electric. In 1890, he told company president Henry Villard that he was retiring from the lighting business, and that he held a greater interest in an iron ore refining project. In October 1890, Edison Machine Works began to develop AC-based equipment, and several Edison subsidiaries began adding AC power transmission to their systems.

By this time, more than 60 patent infringement lawsuits between Edison General Electric and Thomson-Houston were tied up in the courts. President Henry Villard began exploring a means of merging the two rival companies. Once again, Edison opposed the idea, but he lacked the support of the board and was unable to prevent it when Villard explained that Edison General Electric would be in a position to dictate the terms of the merger. The merger would eliminate the patent infringement lawsuits, which were a financial drain for both companies. J.P. Morgan led a committee of financiers who examined the books of both companies, and when Morgan pronounced Thomson-Houston to be the stronger of the two companies financially, he engineered a deal that put management of Thomson-Houston in control of the new company, dropping Edison's name entirely and establishing General Electric.

Only five years earlier, 15 electrical companies had been in existence. With the flurry of Westinghouse's purchases and the final merger of Thomson-Houston and Edison General Electric, there were two — General Electric and Westinghouse. Seventy-five percent of the electrical business of the United States was controlled by General Electric.

Edison's decision to favor direct current over AC current, which he continued doggedly, not only caused him to lose the war of the currents, but also cost him the companies he had founded. Edison continued to hold stock in some General Electric subsidiary companies until 1897. He never publicly retracted his stance during the war of the currents, nor did he apologize for the attacks on Westinghouse.

In 1892, Westinghouse, having successfully demonstrated the universal alternating current system at the Columbian Exposition, was awarded the contract to build the AC power station at Niagara Falls. General Electric was awarded contracts to build transmission lines for that project.

# Edison Emerges Unblemished

The war of the currents was not Thomas Edison's finest hour. Throughout it, he exhibited a dogmatic opposition to the AC system. He engaged in personal attacks on George Westinghouse and Nikola Tesla, and colluded with others to initiate further attacks. He participated financially and publicly in the execution of dogs, cattle, and at least one horse using the AC system in order to help denigrate it in the public eye.

Edison's folly in the war of currents was based on his refusal to adapt his system to accommodate the needs of the public. He believed that the public's demand for electrification would trump the discomforts involved with its generation and distribution. He also believed that the difficulties with providing electrical power to more remote and rural locations could be addressed by further improvements and modifications of the DC system.

Edison's personal records and writings during the war of the currents show that he had a firm understanding of both the advantages and disadvantages of both systems, including the relative safety hazards. He simply could not admit that the system he had favored was inferior. Edison made many faulty business decisions during his career as a manufacturer and industrialist, but his poor decision during the war of the currents was arguably his worst.

Within a few years, he sold his remaining stock in General Electric to support another business venture. Had he retained those shares just a few years longer, they would have made him fabulously wealthy for his day.

Edison's position during the war of the currents did not diminish the esteem in which he was held by the general public. Even while engaged in his attempts to prevent the spread of the clearly superior AC distribution system, he was involved in other projects that enhanced his standing as a Wizard, although no longer at Menlo Park. From his new laboratory in West Orange, Edison had been working on another development which once again spawned an entirely new industry, one that quickly enchanted the world — motion pictures.

# Chapter 4:

# The Flickering Screen

Mary, Edison's first wife, died in August 1884 from unknown causes. In February 1886, 39-year-old Edison married Mina Miller, 19 years his junior, with whom he had another three children; Madeleine born in 1888, Charles, who was born in 1890, and who eventually took over his father's company and laboratories, and Theodore, who eventually graduated from the Massachusetts Institute of Technology and in his lifetime was credited with more than 80 patents.

In the early years at Menlo Park, Edison's children were frequently found in the laboratory and workshops. Despite this, Edison was often an absentee father. Both his frenetic work schedule and irregular hours robbed his children of his attention. After his success with the incandescent lamp, his business demanded that he travel frequently, and train travel ensured that many of his trips were extended in nature.

In his later years, Edison spoke of his sons harshly. Of his eldest son, Edison told a friend, "I never could get him to go to school or work in the laboratory. He is therefore absolutely illiterate scientifically and otherwise." His relationship with William, his second son, was similarly strained. Once, when William's wife Blanche wrote to Edison requesting a loan, he replied, "I see no reason whatever why I should support my son. He has done me no honor and has brought the blush of shame to my cheeks many times."

The death of Edison's first wife brought an end to his association with Menlo Park. After marrying Mina, the couple moved into a new home near Edison's newer and larger laboratory in West Orange New Jersey, which they called Glenmont.

# The Iron Ore Mine

As Edison realized that he was destined to lose the war of the currents, he searched for new ventures. In the 1880s, Edison had experimented with a new means of separating iron ore using magnets. Development of the magnetic iron ore separator began at Menlo Park. When the events of the war of the currents required his attention, however, the project was set aside. With the money that he obtained when he cashed out his interests in General Electric, he purchased an iron mine in northern New Jersey near the town of Ogdensburg, and began constructing a system to process iron ore. Rather than using explosives to break up the chunks of ore — an expensive process, given the cost of dynamite — Edison believed the rock could be crushed by steel rollers, creating smaller pieces from which the iron ore could then be magnetically extracted. Edison, rather than residing at his new home at Glenmont, set up shared quarters with his engineers and technicians in an old farmhouse near the mine site, which they jokingly referred to as "The White House."

The mining project encountered a rash of technical problems. The giant steel rollers crushed the rock, making magnetic extraction difficult. The rock crushers also generated thick dust, which in the humid summer air in northern New Jersey made living conditions difficult. Edison was forced to assign a crew of 17 men to simply control the dust when the living conditions caused him to have personnel retention difficulties at the site. Edison remained at the mine site from Monday until late Saturday, spending only Saturday evening and Sunday at home in Glenmont with his family. He never moved them closer to the operation.

When huge reserves of high-grade iron ore were discovered in northeastern Minnesota — the Mesabi Range — Edison's iron ore experiments were doomed. The ore in Minnesota was near the surface, which made it easily mined, and the deposit was close to shipping facilities on Lake Superior. The plummeting price of iron ore as a result of this discovery made Edison's magnetic extraction methods financially impractical.

Despite this, as in the war of the currents when it was evident that his methods could not compete, he refused to give in, even as he became more and more financially drained. "My Wall Street friends think I cannot make another success, and that I am a back number, hence I cannot raise even $10,000 from them, but I am going to show them that they are very much mistaken," he wrote to a colleague.

Despite the unprofitability of the project, it was not be a complete waste of money, as the steel rollers used to crush the rock were eventually found to have a practical application in another area: the manufacture of Portland cement. Still, it continued to drain his resources and distract his attention from potentially lucrative projects.

# Consumer Demand for Entertainment

Edison's isolation from the public put him out of touch with the mass consumer market. His losses in the mine could be added to the missed opportunities to profit from his other inventions, in particular the phonograph. By the early 1890s, public demand for recorded music was growing. Other inventors had improved upon Edison's phonograph without violating his patents, such as using the medium of revolving discs rather than rotating cylinders. The phonograph was still too expensive for the average family to purchase for the home. Instead, music parlors, where customers could listen to a single recorded selection for the price of a nickel, opened in cities throughout the country. As late as 1892, Edison still opposed the use of the phonograph for entertainment purposes, believing instead that its best use was in offices and businesses for recording dictation.

In the fall of 1888, Edison made his initial foray into the realm of motion pictures, driven partially by an expanded use for his phonograph. That October, he wrote, "I am experimenting upon an instrument which does for the eye what the phonograph does for the ear." As in his earlier work, Edison did not start from scratch, but rather improved the previously completed work of others, in particular an English photographer named

Eadweard Muybridge, a photographer who reached great renown when he took photos in Yosemite.

# The Kinetoscope

With the mining project still demanding his full attention throughout the week, Edison assigned his chief photographer, William L. Dickson, to supervise the project. Despite a slow start, in the summer of 1889 the project took on more urgency. Edison traveled to Paris in August of that year, where he viewed devices using flexible filmstrips. In November, Edison filed a preliminary claim with the US patent office describing a kinetoscope which used a flexible filmstrip perforated on the edge so as to be driven by sprockets. In the spring of 1891, Dickson and Edison were prepared to demonstrate their first prototype kinetoscope. The device was a pine box with a small hole at the top. When the viewer looked through the hole, they saw the image of a man (Dickson) bowing, waving his hands and taking off his hat. According to the New York Sun, "every motion was perfect."

In August, Edison submitted three patent applications for a kinetographic camera, another camera, and for an "Apparatus for Exhibiting Photographs of Moving Objects." Edison had no intention of missing out on the commercial applications for this latest invention as he had for so long with the phonograph. Subsequent design work on the kinetoscope included steps to make it coin-operated as part of the operating viewing system.

That same spring of 1891, Edison visited Chicago to discuss what he would exhibit at the upcoming World's Columbian Exposition. In response to reporters' questions, he announced, "My intention is to have such a happy combination of photography and electricity that a man can sit in his own parlor and see depicted upon a curtain the forms of the players and Opera upon a distant stage and hear the voices of the singers." Edison described a projected viewing and sound system. Since Edison still concentrated on his failing magnetic iron ore extractor, the responsibility for the final development of the kinetoscope was thrust on Dickson. The demands of having the device ready for the Columbian Exposition proved to be too much for Dickson. The kinetoscope — which Edison called the kinetograph — was not ready for public consumption until the following year.

In order to produce the films for viewing on the Kinetograph, Dickson had constructed a movie studio, covered in tarpaper, which he and the workers nicknamed "Black Maria." The studio was mounted on a turntable and equipped with a retractable roof in order to more readily align it with the sun, which provided ample light for filming. As Dickson began creating short films for public consumption, Edison assistant Alfred Tate, recognizing the commercial possibilities his employer did not, purchased a former shoe shop at 1155 Broadway, New York City, and installed in it the first kinetoscope parlor. 10 machines were delivered in April of 1894. These machines were delivered without the coin slots, so Tate issued paper tickets instead — the world's first movie tickets.

On a Saturday afternoon, two days before the planned opening of Tate's kinetoscope parlor, he and his partners opened the doors for an unscheduled preview. Legend has it that they wagered among themselves whether or not they would make enough money to treat themselves to dinner at nearby Delmonico's restaurant. This preliminary opening revealed an almost insatiable demand from the public to see the new moving pictures, and also established the need for Dickson to rapidly create more films, as it was clear the public had no desire to see the same film over and over.

# The Film Projector

Soon Dickson was filming prize fights, and modifying the mechanics of the Kinetograph to accommodate the longer films. A group of entrepreneurs, Otway and Gray Latham and their partner Enoch Rector, began to press Edison to develop a projection system through which all their patrons could simultaneously watch the same film on a large screen, rather than through individual kinetographs. Edison declined. He believed that a projection system would kill the market for the kinetograph, the sales of which were helping to offset his continuing losses in his mining projects. "There will be a use for maybe about 10 of them in the whole United States," he said. "Let's not kill the goose that lays the golden egg." Once again,

Edison failed to recognize the realities of the marketplace, and thus did not achieve the full commercial success of his invention.

Dickson accurately perceived the market for a projection system, and without the knowledge or approval of Edison began working in conjunction with the Lathams on a projection system. When Edison got wind of Dickson's project, he resigned, and the resulting intellectual property issues became the source of litigation which continued for many years.

By the time Edison began to develop a projection system, it was almost too late. Edison would lend his name to a projection system, which he called the Edison-Vitascope, but he had little to do with its development. It was the invention of a Washington DC inventor, Thomas Armat, and his partner Francis Jenkins. When Edison continued to balk at developing a projection system, one of his largest kinetoscope distributors — Raff and Gammon — reviewed Armat's system. Finding it suitable, they arranged with Armat to remove his name from his own invention, and then informed Edison that they intended to purchase the system and abandon the kinetograph.

Faced with the loss of one of his largest customers and sources of income, at a time when he was still bleeding money from his failing mining projects, Edison agreed to the arrangement. The vitascope projected life-size images, and upon its debut in New York was described as the "ingenious inventor's latest toy."

## Edison Movie Studios

The vitascope projection system was an immediate success, adding to Edison's reputation, and creating the new industry of film production. Edison became a studio head. One of his earliest films was entitled Mister Edison at Work in His Chemical Laboratory. Filmed in Dickson's Black Maria, in which a set had been constructed to represent a laboratory, it featured Edison pretending to be engaged in a demanding experiment.

As in previous projects, Edison was credited with the invention of a device and system when the work was largely that of others. Edison also displayed his characteristic stubborn resistance to the reality of market conditions, refusing to abandon his approach in the face of competition from more efficient methods. In the end, his work on the film projection system was negligible, and his company's involvement was limited to that of the efforts of William Dickson, which were conducted without Edison's knowledge or approval. Yet Edison still became known as the inventor of motion pictures, a reputation he built upon when he operated a motion picture studio for several years.

He also failed to appreciate the entertainment value of his invention, and saw it as a tool to be marketed as a training and education device. When the market for business and educational uses did not develop, Edison lost interest in the device until a new technical need arose— the merging of pictures and sound. Still, although the opportunity appeared for a new business dominated by Edison products and enterprises, he turned away from it and remained with a venture which drained his resources and offered little prospect for success.

# Chapter 5:

# The Industrial Giant

In the late 1890s, Thomas Edison obtained a court order to prevent a company doing business as The Edison Chemical Company from using his name. The company, which had no relationship with Edison, had found a man who shared Edison's last name and was willing to license it to the company – an ink manufacturer – for a fee. In response to Edison's injunction, the company hired Thomas Alva Edison Jr. — Edison's son — and reorganized as the Thomas A. Edison Jr. Chemical Company. It also prominently displayed the image of a wizard in its advertising materials. Edison eventually signed an agreement with his son in which the latter agreed to cease marketing his name in consideration of a weekly sum from his father.

Such was the power of Edison's name and reputation with the general public that it conveyed an image of innovation and quality that people wanted to be associated with, regardless of the nature of the business involved. Hundreds of companies bore his name, and they covered a wide gamut of businesses and enterprises. Many of the companies used the name Edison, although he had no direct business connection with their formation and operation. Some of these were connected to Edison through the use of his products, including many local utilities set up to distribute electricity. Throughout the ebb and flow of his business career, his name retained a mystique with the public, who celebrated the man as much as his accomplishments. Edison was aware of this, and worked hard to protect his image. "I'll protect my name if it costs me every dollar in the world I possess," he said.

Edison created businesses of his own throughout his career, to license his patents, manufacture products, build the equipment used to manufacture his products, distribute electricity, foster invention, create motion pictures, conduct mining operations, and manufacture cement. He obtained a controlling interest in previously operating companies and later sold them. Many of these companies merged with each other, and then again with others, and eventually became part of General Electric. Others continued to operate independently in his lifetime, and some existed for decades after his death.

In his business dealings, his greatest strength became his ability to identify and hire individuals who not only possessed great skill and talent, but an ability to absorb their boss's idiosyncrasies and demanding requirements. Some, such as Nikola Tesla, quickly developed a distaste for continuing relations with Edison. Others, such as Charles Batchelor, became lifelong friends.

Throughout the 1870s and 80s, Edison created and operated companies aimed at establishing himself as the dominant producer and distributor of incandescent light. These companies manufactured light bulbs and sockets, wire, transformers, insulators, connectors, and the machines to manufacture them. He established companies to generate current and distribute it to customers. Other companies continued research and development, explored markets, built generating systems and delivery networks, manufactured and installed meters, and collected fees for electric use. These companies had gradually been merged together, and finally became the Edison General Electric Company. In the aftermath of the ill-advised war of the currents, Edison lost control of these companies, along with the patents upon which they were built.

Edison retained a large bloc of General Electric stock, which he began selling to cover the losses sustained by his mining operations, which he was finally forced to shut down for renovation and redesign, a process which became a recurring event. In 1894, Edison sold his remaining General Electric shares, and was retained by the company as a "consultant."

## Edison Manufacturing Company

The need to consolidate his remaining and expanding interests, which were widely varied, drove Edison to establish the Edison Manufacturing Company in 1889. Edison Studios — his motion picture company — became part of Edison Manufacturing. The company manufactured Edison's kinetograph, wax for phonograph cylinders, phonographs, and electric fans, among other products. Chief among these was batteries.

Edison had taken an interest in batteries at least as far back as his development of the ill-fated electric pen, and the design of a Frenchman named Felix Lalande intrigued him. The Lalande battery used powdered copper oxide in liquid. Edison improved this design by replacing the powdered copper oxide with copper oxide briquettes, generating a higher current while retaining its low voltage.

Edison envisioned this battery, and subsequent improvements to it, to be the power source for an electric automobile. He believed that electric cars were the future, rather than the noisier and more dangerous internal combustion engine. At a time when urban streets were still filled with horses, the frequently backfiring, steadily clattering, gas-powered car was a nuisance. The electric car could glide in elegant silence. Improving electric storage cells became Edison's new obsession. Within a few years, he claimed to have developed a car capable of traveling more than eighty miles before needing to recharge the battery at a speed of more than 70 mph.

# The Edison Electric Automobile

Edison's pursuit of an electric car presented many of the same obstacles as his championing of the inferior DC electrical system and his repeated failures in ore extraction. In all three, changing conditions and financial considerations placed him behind events as they transpired, rather than at the forefront. By the time he had developed a workable extraction method for iron ore, it was available far more cheaply than his system could produce. By the time Edison had improved his batteries to the point where they proved a workable alternative to internal combustion, the gas powered automobile had achieved a foothold from which it could not be dislodged, led by a former Edison Illuminating Company of Detroit engineer named Henry Ford.

Henry Ford had first appeared in the Quadricycle, his first automobile, on the streets of Detroit in 1896. At the time, Ford was an employee of the Edison Illuminating Company. Edison encouraged Ford to continue to improve his automobile, but privately he believed the electric car to be the true future of automobiles. "Electricity is the thing," he wrote. "There are no whirring and grinding gears with their numerous levers to confuse. There is not that almost terrifying uncertain throbbing were of the powerful combustion engine. There is no water circulating system to get out of order — no dangerous and evil-smelling gasoline and no noise."

Edison, in a 1914 interview with Automobile Topics, stated about his upcoming electric car, "Mister Henry Ford is making plans for the tools, special machinery, factory buildings and equipment for the production of this new electric. There is so much special work to be done that no date can be fixed now as to when the new electric can be put on the market." Later in the same interview Edison said, "I believe that ultimately the electric motor will be universally based for trucking in all large cities, and that the electric automobile will be the family carriage of the future." But the electric car was never completed; problems with developing suitable batteries prevented work from going forward, and Ford's Model T dominated the market before a practical electric car could be completed.

Edison's fascination with the electric car distracted him from a potentially lucrative commercial enterprise yet again. Consumers desired personal sources of music. Edison had retained the patents on the phonograph, and improvements had continued. They had developed the ability to mass produce pressings of the same recording from a single master copy, and had also created a reliable spring motor for the phonograph. As demand from the public for more phonographs and music cylinders increased, Edison only reluctantly agreed to the expansion of the facilities to produce them. By the end of the first decade of the 20th century, the National Phonograph Company, which contained within its structure Edison Records — one of the earliest record labels — and the Edison Manufacturing Company occupied sixteen buildings in West Orange. Edison, along with Victor and Columbia, dominated the recorded music industry. Still, errors in marketing continued.

# The Music Man

The Edison cylinder, which contained only about two minutes of recorded music, generated about forty-three cents gross profit per unit. This alone was enough to discourage Edison from switching to the more popular disc system used by Victor and Columbia. It also limited his customers' market for new music to that which he produced, while the discs of his competitors were interchangeable. Edison established standards which, even after he had grudgingly given in to producing discs and disc players, ensured that Edison records could only be played on Edison phonographs. When Victor produced an adapter which would enable their machines to play Edison cylinders, Edison directed that no similar system expanding the repertoire of Edison machines be developed.

Curiously, Edison, whose deafness had worsened with age, insisted on final approval of the music that Edison Records offered to its customers. His musical tastes varied, and his opinion of what constituted good music was a strongly held conviction. He despised loud music in all forms, insisting that "anyone who really had a musical ear wanted soft music." However, his deafness made such music difficult to hear. To listen to the music and approve it, he amplified the sound from his phonograph by biting into the wooden box of the device. His teeth and jaw vibrated with the music, which enabled him to hear it better. He preferred waltzes, and because of the technical difficulties corresponding to recording a full orchestra, he preferred those played on a piano.

To solve the difficulties of orchestral recording, he manufactured a brass horn that was over one hundred and twenty-five feet long, five feet in diameter at the receiving end, tapering to about a half an inch at the opposite end. The interior of the horn was smoothed to perfection; even the rivets joining the brass sheets were rendered flush to the surface. It didn't work, however, at least not well enough to enable the sound of an orchestra to be faithfully recorded and reproduced by the much smaller horn connected to the Edison Phonograph. The great horn was eventually donated to a World War I scrap drive for metals.

As his company's musical director, it also fell to Edison to negotiate contracts with artists Edison Records wanted to turn into recording stars, an activity he hated. He believed that most of the artists of the day were motivated not by a love of their art but by the accumulation of wealth. His distaste for the artists meant that Edison Records missed out on signing many of the budding stars of the day, including Fanny Brice and Al Jolson. These and many others were signed by his competition.

Edison also refused to put the name of the artist on recording labels, and when this policy was questioned by one of his dealers, Edison responded in a huff. "Your business has probably not brought you into intimate contact with musicians, but mine has... I would rather quit the business than be a party to the boasting up of undeserved reputations," he replied. To Edison, his fame and the esteem in which the public held him was sufficient to stimulate the sales of his products.

For Edison, the recording business and the phonograph were mere sidelines to his attention. His primary focus at the time was on the development of improved storage batteries to power an electric car that he hoped to market to the masses. He frequently dismissed the complaints of his record dealers and his staff in the recording and phonograph departments as mere annoyances and unnecessary intrusions on his time. He maintained control, but did not wish to invest the time to fully understand and adjust his product lines to meet market demand. He remained supremely confident in his own judgment.

Other sidelines came and went during this period. The Home Projecting Kinetoscope was introduced, but failed to generate much commercial interest. He developed an exchange by which customers could return used films for new ones, swapping titles for a nominal fee. His own opinion was that the projector was best used for educational purposes rather than entertainment, and the films he produced were designed as such.

Edison's primary interest in the music business, the film studio, and his diverse other commercial enterprises was the generation of profit which could be diverted into research money for his work with batteries. In 1912, Edison was approached by the young engineer Henry Ford, formerly employed by Edison Illuminating in Detroit, with a request that Edison design the electrical system for a new car Ford was developing — the Model T. Edison responded with a proposal that Ford provide financial backing for the development of Edison's battery. Their partnership evolved into a close friendship.

## Edison and Ford

Their friendship began with the business relationship in which Ford provided development funds for the battery and they partnered to develop of an Edison-Ford Electric car. It was not long before their families socialized with each other and visited each other's homes in Detroit, Glenmont, and at the vacation home Edison had bought in Ft. Myers, Florida.

The two had much in common besides their technical natures. One of the less fortunate and less widely reported similarity was in their anti-Semitic views.

Ford was virulently anti-Semitic, and waged a long campaign in the press blaming Jews for the world's problems and condemning their "domination" of international finance. Edison tended to keep his thoughts on the subject more private, expressing them in letters to friends and colleagues and in private conversations. Despite this, his anti-Semitism was present in his beliefs and work practices. Author Paul Auster related an incident involving his father. He had been hired by Edison to work in the Orange laboratory, only to be fired immediately after Edison discovered that he was Jewish.

When Ford sent Edison a copy of the anti-Jewish work The International Jew, Edison kept it prominently displayed on his bookshelf, and in subsequent conversations with Ford and others discussed its contents. During the camping trips Edison and Ford took years later, the discussion around the evening campfire often concerned Jews and the perceived problems they caused. John Burroughs recorded many of these conversations in his journals.

Edison believed, according to his own words as written to Isaac Markens, a scholar and writer, that Jewish people excelled in the arts and sciences, but that they provided "some 'terrible examples' in mercantile pursuits." In the same letter, Edison expressed his hope that exposure to American culture and democratic principles would help them eventually "cease to be so clannish."

Edison's motion picture studio produced some films portraying Jews using the stereotypes of the day, including one entitled Cohen's Fire Sale, in which Cohen schemes to commit insurance fraud, and at the end is incapable of kissing his fiancé because of his overly large nose. In another, the same character gives a coat to a tramp. Later it is revealed that the coat bears an advertisement on the back, reading "Go to Cohen's for clothing." The coat was not a charitable gift, but was a self-serving act.

## The Partnership

Edison found in the Ford Motor Company a ready customer for many of his commercial products besides car batteries, generators, and other electrical components. Training films were produced for use in Ford's factories, and projecting equipment was sold to display them. Modified phonographs in the form of Edison Dictating Machines were soon found in Ford offices. One of the most lucrative arrangements was in the contracts for the cement to be used in the construction for all buildings of the rapidly expanding Ford Motor Company. It was supplied by the Edison Portland Cement Company.

The Edison-Ford electric car partnership did not produce a marketable electric car. Before the project dissolved, Henry Ford invested more than $1.5 million in it and had purchased almost 100,000 batteries from Edison. Edison was unable to solve the problem of the high internal resistance within the batteries, which rendered them incapable of generating enough power to move a car.

Ford's motives for partnering with Edison are unknown, as an electric car would directly compete with his own Model T. It is possible that Ford used the joint project as a means to fund Edison under the guise of mutual research. Henry Ford worshipped Thomas Edison, referring to him many times as, "the greatest man in the world." Edison badly needed funding for both his storage battery projects and the failing iron ore extraction project. Ford's funds may have actually been intended to help his friend and one-time mentor alleviate his financial difficulties.

# Edison Portland Cement Company

The Edison Portland Cement Company was an outgrowth of Edison's mining activities. The huge rollers which Edison had created for the purpose of crushing rocks produced very fine waste sand, which was useful in the production of Portland cement, a critical ingredient of concrete. Beginning in 1899, Edison established the Edison Portland Cement Company to exploit this potential market, and began to explore new uses for concrete. He proposed houses built entirely from concrete with prefabricated walls, and even proposed furniture manufactured from concrete, which he suggested could be dyed to resemble wood, and installed as a permanent part of the structure. These announcements met with wide spread derision amongst the media, especially as far as the furniture was concerned.

Edison erected concrete structures to house his film and music companies, eventually expanding his complex at West Orange to eighteen buildings surrounding his laboratory, all of concrete, which Edison presented to the public as "absolutely fireproof." Although the structures of the buildings was fireproof, the materials contained within them were highly flammable. In December of 1914, a fire began in one of the buildings, and, fed by the stocks of film and vast collection of chemicals, it soon destroyed the internal structural supports that held up the concrete walls, which collapsed under their own weight. The heat spread the fire to other buildings, and by the end of the long night, ten buildings of the Edison complex were destroyed, along with their contents. Edison's confidence that his complex was immune to the threat of fire had led him to underinsure the buildings. The losses, estimated to be as high as $5 million, were insured for less than $3 million. Edison maintained his usual aplomb, commenting that despite his age of 67, he would "start all over again tomorrow."

Edison sometimes demonstrated a lack of understanding for the basics of economics. For example, the Edison Portland Cement Company developed a rotary kiln for the production of cement, which led to increased production far beyond the demand for the product, lowering prices and causing operating losses. Besides the sale of its products to the

Ford Motor Company, Edison's cement was used in roads, dams, and large buildings, but neither the pre-cast concrete home market nor the proposed furniture business ever got off the ground, though Edison built some prototype concrete homes in New Jersey. The company operated at a loss until 1922, when Edison won the contract to provide the cement for the construction of Yankee Stadium in the Bronx. There his concrete proved to be so durable that, when the stadium was renovated in 1973, it was determined that there was no need for any modifications or renovations on the areas of the stadium built with it. The concrete remained in place until the stadium was demolished in 2008.

The friendship between Edison and Ford flourished, but Edison's businesses that supplied the Ford Motor Company did not. Supplying a reliable battery for commercial use in a Ford car proved difficult. The batteries provided to Ford drained too quickly, failed to re-charge when the car was running, and provided limited power to headlights. Edison excused these failings through his secretaries and assistants, who explained to their counterparts at Ford that his attention had been directed by events to the phonograph and film businesses, and that he could then give his full attention to the Ford needs. Still, the batteries failed to meet Ford's expectations and Edison's promises.

When the 1914 fire destroyed much of Edison's complex, Henry Ford immediately offered both personal and company support to Edison. But by this time Ford had decided that the Edison alkaline battery was insufficient for use in Ford cars, which he marketed under the twin benefits of affordability and reliability. The decision by Ford did not alter the personal relationship between the two men, as Ford provided hundreds of thousands of dollars in loans to the Edison Company, the bulk of which were forgiven unpaid.

# Diversification and Public Image

Edison created Thomas A. Edison, Incorporated in 1911. The Edison Manufacturing Company was restructured as a division, and Edison took over as president and chairman in December of 1912. This company served as the holding company for Edison's diverse interests. Throughout his career, Edison established hundreds of companies and acquired controlling interest in others in the United States and Europe to advance his businesses. He manufactured and sold phonographs, small appliances, telegraph and telephone equipment, electric fans, batteries, radios, and electric machinery. He produced and sold concrete and concrete products. He produced and sold motion pictures, along with projection equipment and motion picture cameras. He sold automobile batteries and generators, and established garages to service cars equipped with his products.

Although he achieved considerable wealth as a result of these ventures and was considered by the public to be an industrial titan, he never achieved the wealth of some of his contemporaries, with whom he was friends. His relationships with Henry Ford, Harvey Firestone, (Firestone Tire and Rubber), John Patterson (National Cash Register), and even Presidents Harding and Coolidge, with whom he vacationed, cemented his image as a leading industrialist, which was largely false.

Edison's public image remained untarnished because he was credited with inventing the electric light, the phonograph, motion pictures and many others that continued to improve and become more affordable. His public association with the industrial titans who advanced great changes through their products allowed him to share their limelight, despite the failure of his fitful contributions to the automotive industry. Edison was not their equal as a businessman, but neither were they his equal in the mind of a public that still regarded Edison with awe as the Wizard of Menlo Park.

Throughout the many difficulties Edison endured, Henry Ford remained one of his staunchest supporters and promoters. Ford downplayed problems with Edison's products to the press, and continued to speak of Edison with respect. Edison was by then many years removed from a major success both in the laboratory and in business, but because of his association with Ford he remained in the public eye a great inventor, shrewd businessman, and one of the industrial giants of the age.

Edison continued to work on an electric starter for Ford until Charles Kettering beat him to it in 1915. He worked on improved batteries, generators and lighting systems, many of which failed to deliver on his promise. His association with Ford continued for the rest of his life, but his contributions to the automobile industry were minor.

# Chapter 6:

# The Public Man

In August of 1914, World War I broke out in Europe. The United States immediately declared its neutrality. American newspapers carried lurid stories about German atrocities in Belgium and the horrible new weapons of war that were deployed. German submarines sank British merchant ships with relative impunity. The airplane — just over a decade old — became a potent new weapon against troops on the ground and against each other. Machine guns and massive cannons deployed against troops soon caused the armies on all fronts to burrow into the ground. Trench warfare stretched across Europe.

In May of 1915, Thomas Edison granted an interview to the New York Times in which he addressed the European war and America's role in the changing world. He advocated the construction of machines to prepare America for modern warfare, but not the creation of an army to use them. Instead, he proposed that ships and weapons be assembled and stored for future use, acknowledging the inevitability of America's eventual involvement in armed conflict. "I believe that the developments of the European war have proved beyond a shadow of a doubt the uselessness of large standing armies," he said. "We should not take our men from industry and over train them, but we should have 2 million rifles ready, in perfect order, even greased, with armories equipped with the very best machinery to begin upon short notice, in case the work should be required, the manufacture of 100,000 new firearms every day."

## The Naval Control Board

Edison called for maintaining the current manning levels authorized by the U.S. Congress— an army of 100,000 men— but preparing for a potential emergency by having equipment designed, built, and stored. He also called for nationalizing the individual states' militia. "What we want is a small army trained to a big knowledge, and trained to teach it as well as to exercise it... We have many millions of potential fighting men."

Edison's interview drew the attention of Secretary of the Navy Josephus Daniels, who wrote Edison in July and asked him to gather a panel of experts to consult with the U.S. Navy. When this panel formally convened in October 1915, Edison was elected chairman, and the panel took the formal name the "Naval Consulting Board." Edison's personal assistant on the board was his chief engineer, Miller Reese Hutchison. Hutchison had actually proposed the board to Secretary Daniels, and hoped to equip the U.S. Navy's growing submarine fleet with Edison storage batteries.

While he served on the Naval Consulting Board, Edison remained involved with his companies, and decisions made by the board directly affected his business. While this practice may be viewed as a conflict of interest, it was common at the time. Edison's recommendations to the Naval Consulting Board on the number and types of ships to be constructed had a direct correlation to the number of storage batteries that he could sell. It also offered Edison insights into other industries affected by the war, and to the shortages of materials which would result in the United States by the disruption of European markets and shipping.

Prior to the outbreak of the war, many of the chemicals used in American industry had been imported from both Germany and England, who were busy enthusiastically sinking each other's merchant fleets. Edison responded to the resulting shortage by creating new chemical manufacturing plants, and he became a major supplier to the European allies and American industry. When carbolic acid — which was needed to manufacture Edison's phonograph records — became hard to find, Edison built a carbolic acid plant, and had it in operation in only 17 days. Similarly, Edison established plants in Johnstown, Pennsylvania and Woodward, Alabama to manufacture benzol, also required for his phonograph and for military use.

In early 1917, Edison established a new laboratory in West Orange New Jersey for the specific purpose of research into military requirements and developments. As German submarines continued to wreak havoc upon Britain's merchant fleet, Edison worked on developing methods to evade torpedoes. He and his assistants worked on sensitive sound equipment, ship telephone systems, devices to determine the location of heavy guns, and devices for the detection of submarine periscopes. In late 1917, Edison worked for a time at the Navy Annex in Washington DC, and later at the US Naval Station, Key West, Florida. He continued this work after the United States became involved in the war in 1917, and before the war was over, he had proposed 48 separate inventions, none of which were accepted by the US War Department nor the Department of the Navy.

Edison was equally unsuccessful in the sale of his storage batteries for use in US submarines. During early testing, the battery demonstrated a tendency to overheat and explode during charging and quickly became distrusted by the submarine builders and the Navy Department, despite Secretary Daniels's support. Other Edison batteries found customers in the manufacturers of the industrial trucks which replaced the horse-drawn wagons in the Allied armies' logistics chains. The batteries were also used in surface ships, field radios, other vehicles, and forward position communication sites.

Edison had no military experience or training, but his comments in the New York Times interview were somewhat prophetic. When the United States entered the war, it had a small professional army, but it rapidly expanded and trained an expeditionary force that was sent to Europe. Materially unprepared for the war, US pilots flew French airplanes, and US artillery units were equipped with French guns. But the massive army which Edison had foretold was quickly assembled in response to the emergency as predicted, and helped turn the tide of the war.

# Leaving the Motion Picture Business

Throughout his professional career, Edison was embroiled in patent suits brought against him and those he filed against others. One of these, between his Motion Picture Patents Company and the Universal Film Manufacturing Company, was decided by the US Supreme Court in April 1917. That decision made Edison's licensing agreements illegal. In the wake of this suit, Edison decided to abandon the motion picture business, selling his film studio to the Lincoln and Parker Film Company in 1918. When that firm went bankrupt in 1919, Edison reacquired his assets and resold them to film producer Robert L Giffen in October of that year.

Edison departed the motion picture business a mere five years after he introduced another technology which changed the industry forever – talking motion pictures. He accomplished the synchronized soundtrack by linking a phonograph with pulleys to a film projector, a device which he called the kinetophone. Although Edison invented what would become known in the industry and the public as "talkies," he preferred silent pictures, possibly due to his worsening deafness.

# The Vagabonds

By 1914, Henry Ford's success with his automobile was reflected by hundreds of thousands of Americans touring the country, an opportunity provided by his affordable cars. Ford and Edison embarked on a trip to Florida's Everglades that winter, the first of several camping trips that took place over the following decade. On their first trip, they were accompanied by John Burroughs, an essayist and naturalist who named the campers the "Vagabonds."

The camping excursions served as publicity opportunities for Ford automobiles and trucks. They included a caravan of Ford vehicles, which carried provisions and gear. The men were also accompanied with a support staff, including drivers, mechanics, cooks, and servants, and photographers and film crews were brought along to record the events. By 1919, Fort designed a special kitchen car equipped with a gasoline stove and an ice box. That year's trip included 50 vehicles.

Over several trips, notable industrialists and influential people joined Ford and Edison. Tire magnate Harvey Firestone, Executive of the United States Shipping Board Edward Hurley, and Professor RJ DeLoach, a leading expert in botany and plant pathology accompanied them on various trips. In 1921, President Warren G.

Harding joined them, as he was a good friend of Firestone's.

The 1923 trip included a visit to President Coolidge, who had succeeded Harding, at his home in Massachusetts. In April of 1924, the group toured the Upper Peninsula of Michigan. Ford commissioned a special train for the trip. He acted as engineer and Harvey Firestone served as the fireman as they toured several Ford properties.

According to Burroughs, the group as a whole would "cheerfully endure wet, cold, smoke, mosquitoes, black flies, and sleepless nights, just to touch naked reality once more."

Henry Ford plainly enjoyed the trips, and particularly relished the opportunity to repair one of the Packards that had broken down in front of a mechanic who had advised him that it could not be done. Both Ford and Edison enjoyed bathing in streams near their campsites, although the fastidious Firestone preferred showering at a nearby hotel whenever possible. Edison spent much of his time gathering rocks and breaking them with a hammer, examining any ore they contained.

The photographers and film makers that accompanied them ensured that the nation was aware of their travels. Theaters displayed short films of Ford, Burroughs, Edison, and Firestone performing planned hijinks, including foot races against each other, chopping down trees, climbing trees, and on one occasion Edison kicking a cigar off a fireplace mantel three consecutive times. He was 71 at the time. The much younger Ford only accomplished the feat once.

In his autobiography My Life and Work, Henry Ford wrote, "the trips were good fun except that they began to attract too much attention."

Edison never recorded his thoughts about the trips, though his daughter Madeline said that "he would let himself be taken into these things." In Madeline's estimation, her father had not enjoyed the trips. The 1924 trip was the last for a number of reasons, including the press of business on both Ford and Firestone, and the fact that one of the original Vagabonds – Burroughs – had died in 1921. Ford, Firestone, and Edison became known to the public as the "Millionaires Club."

# Philanthropy

Unlike Henry Ford, Harvey Firestone, and indeed many other business magnates of the time, Edison did not involve himself in philanthropic activities. He did not establish an Edison foundation, nor did he support any particular charitable causes as most of his contemporaries with the time and the means did. Part of the reason for this was that Edison never truly retired, nor did he ever intend to.

In 1929, Henry Ford established an endowment of $5 million for the Ford Museum's Edison collection, and created a technical institute named for him. Ford entirely rebuilt the Menlo Park laboratory to honor Edison on the 50th anniversary of the incandescent light bulb. Amongst those present at its dedication were President Herbert Hoover, J.P. Morgan, Orville Wright, and noted humorist Will Rogers. A live radio broadcast of the event was heard nationwide. On this occasion Edison delivered a public speech — a rare event for him — in which he said of Henry Ford, "I can only say to you that in the fullest and richest meaning of the term, he is my friend. Good night."

# Edison Dies at 84

In January of 1931, Edison filed his last patent application for a "Holder for Article to be Electroplated." It was his 1093rd patent. By then, his health was failing. He had long suffered from diabetes. In August of that year, he suffered from kidney failure, and after partially recovering from that crisis, his health rapidly declined. By early autumn, he passed in and out of a coma. On October 17th, he woke from his coma briefly, told his attendant wife that, "it is very beautiful over there," and drifted off once more. He died on October 18, 1931, at the age of 84, at his home in Glenmont.

Henry Ford refused to enter the laboratory library where Edison's bier was open to public visitation, and insisted that he wanted his final memory of Edison to be the last conversation they had held in the same room. An estimated 40,000 visitors paid their respects on the day before his funeral, which was held on the 52nd anniversary of the patent for the incandescent light bulb. The First Lady, Lou Hoover, attended on behalf of her husband, who was unable to attend due to a pending visit from the Premier of France. Ford attended, as did Harvey Firestone.

President Hoover urged all Americans to extinguish their lights at ten p.m. as a tribute, saying, "This demonstration of the dependence of the country upon electrical current for its life and health is in itself a monument to Mr. Edison's genius." As this was before Daylight Savings Time was implemented, Americans responded more or less simultaneously, and the nation went dark for one minute. Edison was buried in Rosedale Cemetery in West Orange, beneath a large oak.

At the time of his death, Edison's estate was estimated to be around $12 million. By the time his will was probated, during the height of the depression, his estate had been reduced to about $1.5 million. His surviving companies did not fare well either, and Thomas A. Edison, Inc. eventually merged with the McGraw Electric Company of Chicago, becoming McGraw-Edison. That company was later taken over by Cooper Industries.

The size of Edison's estate was paltry compared to those of his friends. Henry Ford originally endowed the Ford Foundation with $109 million, and his personal estate was over $70 million at the time of his death. Ford, Firestone, and Edison had been called "the Millionaires Club," but Edison was a very junior member of that club. Most of the money he made went back into his industries, or to businesses that eventually failed. Throughout his career, he invested his successes in order to support his failures. The public perception of him as a tremendous financial success was largely incorrect.

# Chapter 7:

# Edison's Legacy

Thomas Edison was a stubborn man. In many ways, this stubbornness served him well, as it drove him to persist in the face of many failures while striving to complete an invention. In other ways, it harmed him irreparably, as in his stubborn insistence to continue enterprises that were clearly failing. "The most certain way to succeed is always to try just one more time," he famously said, but applying this adage to his own behavior highlights his failures in the mining industry, the rubber industry, and the war of the currents.

Edison was also a determined man, and this determination frequently got him into financial difficulty. He was determined that his phonograph should be used as a business and educational tool, and his films for education. When the public exhibited more frivolous uses for his inventions, he backed away from them rather than indulge what he perceived to be undisciplined pursuits. He believed that his taste in music was superior to those who had differing tastes, and that if he limited music recording to that which he approved, the public would be brought around to see things his way. When the public simply bought his competitors' offers, he refused to alter this thinking.

## Patents and Lawsuits

Of Edison's 1093 US patents, more than half were concerned with either electrical lighting or phonographs and recording. The large majority of his patents were for improvements or minor adjustments for patents he already owned, and nearly all of them were in his name, although significant research and development work had been done by his employees and assistants. Edison received patents overseas as well, and while an accurate account is difficult to measure, the 1910 biography Edison: His Life and Inventions claimed he held 1,239 overseas patents in 34 countries. These were often on the same subject matter as his US patents. Edison applied for and either withdrew or was denied an additional 500-600 patents.

The sheer number of patents issued in his name led Edison to spend most of his life involved in suits and countersuits. These suits often led to monumentally bad business decisions and diverted financial resources which could have been put to better use elsewhere. It was one such suit that finally led Edison to abandon the motion picture industry just as it stood on the doorstep of its Golden Age. When motion pictures exploded as a form of entertainment in the Roaring Twenties, Edison had left the industry behind, separating himself from what could have been vast profits to feed his other endeavors. Similarly, he abandoned the recording industry just as radio entered its heyday as the leading in-home entertainment medium.

# Menlo Park and Henry Ford

Henry Ford deserves much of the credit for Edison's enduring legacy. Ford re-created the Menlo Park laboratory and Edison's home at a site near Detroit, dedicating it on October 21, 1929 to coincide with the 50th anniversary of Edison's incandescent light bulb. For the first several years, the complex which Ford named The Edison Institute was used for educational purposes. Later it was opened to the public. Visitors can still see the small laboratory at the Henry Ford Museum, including the workbenches where Edison's team gradually solved the mysteries of a practical incandescent light bulb.

Ford did much to promote Edison and his work during Edison's lifetime, beyond the awarding of contracts for components in his automobiles. He provided loans to a cash-strapped Edison struggling with his iron ore mining ventures, which later became gifts when Edison couldn't meet payments, and Ford forgave the loans. It was Ford who first suggested the camping trips, for which he provided employees to report on and film the travels of the Vagabonds, films which were soon shown in theaters across the country. While it is true that this promoted the Ford brand, he equally promoted the Edison brand at a time when Edison had been long separated from a major success.

Indeed, after the phonograph and the electric light bulb, Edison's only remaining major success had been in motion pictures. Yet even that claim to fame was contested in his lifetime until he finally tired of the battle and withdrew from the business.

# Edison's Mean Streak

Edison's behavior during the war of the currents tarnishes his legacy as well, not only because he championed the wrong system. Had his DC system prevailed, electrification of rural areas would have been long delayed, and may not have been possible at all in more remote locations. His refusal to recognize this and to explore ways to implement the AC system within his own companies was driven both by business interests and by his obstinately held belief that the DC system was superior. When it became clear that that he was wrong, he refused to admit it and resorted instead to personal attacks on George Westinghouse, Nikola Tesla, and others. These personal attacks exhibited a meanness on his part that did him little credit. He supported tests which demonstrated the potential dangers of AC, championed and even wrote propaganda against it, and failed to demonstrate a means by which DC could compete effectively against Westinghouse's system. He stubbornly clung to his conviction that he was right long after the scientific and engineering data established that he was wrong.

## Edison and Tesla

Edison's greatest public image remains that he was the inventor of electric light. By the time Edison approached the subject, more than two dozen working electric light bulbs had been demonstrated, and numerous patents were previously issued. Edison instead made the impractical electric light practical through the use of extensive trial and error, developing a filament which burned brightly enough to generate sufficient light and long enough to eliminate too frequent replacements of the bulb. He developed most of the infrastructure to make incandescent light available to homes and businesses.

An enduring element of the Tesla – Edison feud is that Edison used his position on the Naval Consulting Board during World War I to turn down a pitch from Tesla in which Tesla proposed tracking targets using radio waves — radar. This aspect of Edison's legacy — that he turned down Tesla as partial revenge for the war of the currents — is still espoused by Tesla supporters. Whether Edison had any part in the decision to reject Tesla's pitch is unclear. What is clear is that Tesla's proposal described radar as a means of tracking submarines. Experts on the Naval Consulting Board decided that the radio waves would be attenuated by seawater to the point that they would be unable to track submarines. The Board continued to pursue tracking submarines via sound waves in a sonar device that was likewise being pursued by the British. Whether Tesla's proposal was declined for technical or personal reasons remains unclear to this day, though the official record cites technical limitations.

# Edison's Failures

Many of Edison's more famous quotations reflect his tenacity. "I have not failed. I've just found 10,000 ways that won't work." Another is, "Many of life's failures are people who did not realize how close they were to success when they gave up." When his numerous business failures and poor business decisions are examined with this attitude in mind, those failures are readily explained. Edison refused to believe that his magnetic ore separator would not work and struggled to find the means to perfect it. While he was doing so, the price of iron ore dropped below the point at which his business would have failed even if his separator functioned properly. Edison did not allow this fact to dissuade him from continuing work on the separator. His focus on his clearly unprofitable iron ore business distracted his attention from both the phonograph and music businesses at a time when they were poised to generate enormous profits had he positioned himself to do so.

Despite these failures, Edison continued to believe that his business judgment was sound and his decisions were correct. Those who opposed him were dispensed with in short order. Many went on to enormous success of their own. Many are virtually unknown today, though their contributions partially led to Edison's fame, which endures. One of these was Samuel Insull, who disagreed with Edison during the war of the currents, and who became a leading proponent of the network broadcasting systems as they evolved, as well as the electrification of the city of Chicago. Frank Sprague worked for Edison before forming his own company, the Sprague Electric Railway and Motor Company, which led him to become known as the father of electric traction. Sprague developed the first successful large electrical street railway by connecting his electric cars to an overhead wire via a spring-loaded pole, a technology still used in streetcars as they enjoy a comeback in American cities.

The technologies developed by individuals who had worked in Edison's employ early in their careers – including Nikola Tesla – continue to be used in technology today, and form a part of Edison's legacy.

# Identifying Cigarettes as Harmful

Edison was also one of the earliest persons to identify the harmful effects of cigarette smoking, encouraged in large part by Henry Ford, who despised the habit. Edison himself enjoyed both cigars and chewing tobacco, but hated cigarettes. He wrote, "The injurious agent in cigarettes comes principally from the burning paper wrapper. The substance thereby formed is called 'Acrolein.'...It has a violent action on the nerve centers, producing degeneration of the cells of the brain, which is quite rapid among boys. I employ no person who smokes cigarettes." Edison installed in his plants and workshops signs which read "Cigarettes Not Tolerated. They Dull The Brain." Despite the signs and his insistence, Edison did not exclude cigarette smokers from his plants, but he did discourage their smoking. When he came under attack in newspapers — some of whose largest advertisers were tobacco companies — he responded by establishing his credentials from observing the properties of paper filaments during his extensive research for the light bulb.

Edison claimed that no other person had the expertise with the chemical properties of burning papers that he did. This did not stop the editorials from describing him as straying from his areas of expertise in discussions of the subject. Edison did not demonstrate any harmful effects from tobacco itself, merely from the paper used to make cigarettes. Nonetheless, it was more than 50 years before the Surgeon General of the United States corroborated Edison's findings, identifying harmful materials in both the tobacco and the paper used to make cigarettes.

# Edison's Products and Businesses

Edison was born in 1847, in a nation which had not yet fought its Civil War, not yet tamed the west, and had not yet assumed the mantle of world power. During his lifetime, railroads grew to maturity, steam overtook sail as the means of moving ships, wood was displaced by coal, and was eventually replaced by oil. Labor unions were born, went through a painful period of growth, and then rapidly gained strength. Working conditions and communications both improved. Some of the messages which Edison received and passed along as a telegrapher were news of important battles in Virginia, Tennessee, and Pennsylvania during the Civil War, the assassination of Abraham Lincoln, and the manhunt for his murderer. By the time Edison began his camping expeditions with Ford and Firestone, the telegram had been supplanted by the telephone, and wireless telegrams were more common. Wireless communication between ships and the shore were established.

Western Union continued to dominate the telegraph industry in the United States throughout Edison's life and beyond, using his inventions in multiplex messaging for decades. But with the advent of the telephone, its primary business shifted to the wired transfer of money. Edison's earliest inventions served the industry well into the 21st century, when in 2006 Western Union discontinued telegrams for communication entirely.

Edison's phonograph, and the recording industry it spawned, has become marginalized, yet still endures in subcultural niches. While music is freely available from dozens of sources not visualized by Edison, many audiophiles still believe that recorded music sounds best when heard from a vinyl disc, upon which a needle senses the irregularities in its grooves and reproduces them as vibrations, sensed by electromagnets and converted to electrical signals — the same technology developed by Edison at Menlo Park.

Edison's carbon transmitter was the standard for telephone headsets into the 1980s, when it was eventually replaced with newer technology. Older telephone sets still in use are equipped with the technology he developed. It is destined to vanish over time, as cellular and digital land lines gradually displace it, but it has served well for the 140 years it has been in use.

By the 21st century, the incandescent light bulb was under attack as outdated technology, wasteful of energy, and expensive to manufacture and use. Fluorescent and LED technologies have been deemed to be more energy efficient, less hostile to ecology, and longer lasting than Edison's incandescent bulb. As the 21st century goes on, the incandescent bulb will follow many of Edison's inventions into the archives of history. Ironically, the bulbs which will replace Edison's incandescent light are the result of research into improving it, conducted by research and development facilities, the very practice that Edison followed throughout his life and career.

# Research and Development

The research and development laboratory, an organization designed for the purpose of dedicated exploration into a subject with the intent of improving it, is Thomas Edison's greatest legacy. Edison's "Invention Factories," first at Menlo Park and later in West Orange, were the forerunners of today's research and development departments in large corporations, centers of academia, government facilities, and independent organizations. Edison's design of the inventive process is followed in the areas of pharmaceutical and disease research, aviation, space exploration, automotive design, weapons development, agriculture, civil engineering, and virtually every other discipline.

Just as he rendered the gas lamp obsolete, one day his achievements in lighting will be so rendered. His films can be watched online, using technology of which he could not have dreamed. But his process, including brainstorming, working on multiple projects simultaneously, sharing information between projects, applying multiple solutions and selecting that which worked the best, hiring brilliant talent and then turning them loose to do the work — this and more is the legacy that will far outlast his inventions.

# Edison's Religious Views

In an interview with the New York Times in 1910, Edison was quoted as saying, "Nature is what we know. We do not know the gods of religions. And nature is not kind, or merciful, or loving. If God made me – the fabled God of the three qualities of which I spoke – mercy, kindness, love – He also made the fish I catch and eat. And where do His mercy, kindness, and love for that fish come in? No; nature made us. Nature did it all, not the gods of the religions." This and similar comments he made throughout his life caused the general belief that he was an atheist. Edison denied that he was an atheist in private letters, but refused to enter a public discussion of his personal beliefs.

In 1904, a group of Edison's friends created an award in his name — the Edison Medal — to be awarded by the Institute of Electrical and Electronics Engineers as acknowledgement of a career "of meritorious achievement in electrical science, electrical engineering, or the electric arts." The first recipient was Elihu Thomson in 1909, founder of the Thomson-Houston Electric Company that had merged with Edison General Electric to form General Electric. In 1911, the Edison Medal was awarded to his nemesis in the war of the currents, George Westinghouse, and five years later, Nikola Tesla was also honored. Several of Edison's former employees received the award over time, for work accomplished after leaving his employ.

The day after Edison's death, Nikola Tesla was quoted in the New York Times, saying, "If Edison had a needle to find in a haystack, he would proceed at once with the diligence of the bee to examine straw after straw until he found the object of his search... I was a sorry witness of such doings, knowing that a little theory and calculation would have saved him ninety per cent of his labor."

Tesla may have been a bit unkind in his comment. Edison's legacy is that he achieved his greatest successes by the unrelenting labor of his teams in pursuit of his goals. Yet Edison to some extent would have likely agreed with Tesla's comment, having once told Theodore Dreiser, "When I have fully decided that a result is worth getting, I go about it, and make trial after trial, until it comes." Edison added, "I

hope I will be able to work right on to the close.
I shouldn't care to loaf."

# Epilogue

Thomas Edison's main concern was invention, not financial gain, as shown when he only reluctantly allowed his phonograph and his kinetoscope to be commercialized for the purpose of entertainment. It was his firm belief that the phonograph's future was in business as a means of recording dictation, and that the kinetoscope should be used for the purposes of education and training. He sold his good friend Henry Ford on both of these ideas, and both inventions became part of the Ford Motor Company's training programs. Only after observing the large profits attained by his competitors did he allow his inventions to be exploited for entertainment.

Yet he consistently denied that he was driven by financial considerations, despite this evidence. "One might think that the money value of an invention constitutes its reward to the man who loves his work. But speaking for myself, I can honestly say this is not so... I continue to find my greatest pleasure, and so my reward, in the work that precedes what the world call success." In his own words, his work was its own compensation, and he his lifestyle followed this insistence.

It was Edison's destiny to be known to posterity as the man who brought electric light to the world. Although many were working on the problem of the practical light bulb, it was he who got there first— or maybe he wasn't. Maybe Joseph Swan's light bulb preceded Edison's. Maybe it doesn't really matter. Edison's life and legacy can be summed up simply, in his own words:

"I find out what the world needs," he said. "Then I go ahead and try to invent it."

# Sources

The Edison Papers. Rutgers University
edison.rutgers.edu

The Henry Ford Museum.
www.thehenryford.org/museum

The Thomas Edison Center at Menlo Park.
www.menloparkmuseum.org

The Early Motion Picture and Sound
Recordings of the Edison Companies. Library
of Congress Collection. www.loc.gov/edison

Thomas Edison National Historical Park.
www.nps.gov/edis

Lighting a Revolution: 19th Century
Promotion. The Smithsonian Institution.
americanhistory.si.edu/lighting/19thcent/pro
mo19.htm

Dyer, Frank and Commerford, Martin, Edison: His Life and Inventions. Project Gutenberg. Updated January 26th, 2013.

Stross, Randall, The Wizard of Menlo Park. 2007, Crown Publishers, New York

Dreiser, Theodore, A Photographic Talk with Edison, Success Magazine, February 1898. Available as a PDF nationalhumanitiescenter.org

Tesla, Nikola My Inventions: The Autobiography of Nikola Tesla. 1919 Electrical Experimenter Magazine.

Moran, Richard, Executioner's Current: Thomas Edison, George Westinghouse, and the Invention of the Electric Chair 2007 Random House

Lightning Source UK Ltd.
Milton Keynes UK
UKOW03f1902210417
299663UK00001B/15/P